Journeys

Direct Instruction Reading

Level 2

Textbook 1

Siegfried Engelmann

Owen Engelmann

Karen Lou Seitz Davis

Ann Arbogast

SRA

A Division of The McGraw-Hill Companies

Columbus, Ohio

Illustration Credits

Shirley Beckes, Dave Blanchette, Olivia Cole, Mark Corcoran, Susan DeMarco, John Edwards and Associates, Pat Faessler, Kersti Frigell, Meryl Henderson, Gay W. Holland, Susan Jerde, Anne Kennedy, Loretta Lustig, Jan Pyk, Pat Schories, Jim Shough, Lauren Simeone, Rachel Taylor, and Gary Undercuffler.

SRA/McGraw-Hill

A Division of The **McGraw·Hill** *Companies*

Printed in the United States of America.

Send all inquiries to:
SRA/McGraw-Hill
250 Old Wilson Bridge Road, Suite 310
Worthington, OH 43085

ISBN 0-02-683534-7

1 2 3 4 5 6 7 8 9 VHJ 03 02 01 00 99

ar   oo   al

1. agree
2. between
3. away
4. saving
5. opened

1. m**oo**se
2. t**al**l
3. f**oo**d
4. **al**so

1. stay
2. shark
3. near
4. tail

1. smile
2. named
3. hide
4. close
5. came
6. know

A Clam Named Ann

Clams seem to have a big smile, but some clams are not happy. One sad clam was named Ann. Why was she sad? She did not like to stay in the sand with the other clams.

Ann said, "Why can't I swim with the otters?"

Her mom said, "That's silly. Otters eat clams. They don't swim with clams."

One day, a shark was swimming near the clams. A little otter was swimming near the clams, too. The otter did not see that shark. As the otter came closer, Ann opened her shell and yelled, "Shark, shark. Hide, hide."

The otter hid, and the shark went away.

The next day, the otter came back. She said to the clam, "Thank you for saving me. What can I do in return?"

You know what Ann said, and you know what they did.

So if you ever see an otter swimming with a clam on its tail, you will know who they are.

oo ol ir or

1. zoo
2. goose
3. room
4. broom

1. beach
2. first
3. dark
4. small
5. seal

1. first
2. small
3. seal
4. dark
5. beach

1. Beth
2. Tim
3. none
4. slowly
5. blowing
6. okay

1. scare
2. hates
3. knees
4. yelling

3

A Swim for Bob
Part One

Bob can swim like a seal. None of his pals can
swim well. Tim can not swim at all. Beth can swim,
but she hates to swim. And Beth swims very slowly.
One day Bob was with Beth and Tim. Bob said,
"Why don't we go for a swim at the beach? We can
have fun in the waves."

Tim said, "Not me. I don't like to go near big waves."

Beth said, "I hate to swim."

"Come on," Bob said. "We will have lots of fun in the waves."

At first, Bob's pals didn't feel like going with him. But after a while, they said, "Okay. We will go with you."

Before Bob went swimming, he had to ask his dad. He said, "Let us take the van and go for a swim in the waves."

His dad said, "Okay. But you must be home before it gets dark."

"Yes," Bob said. "We will be back by then."

More to come.

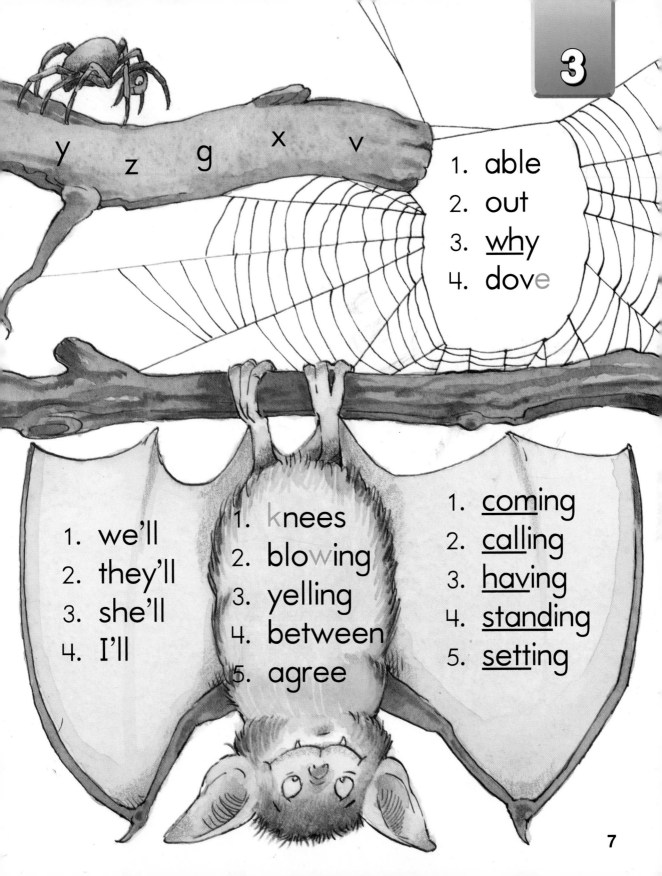

y   z   g   x   v

1. able
2. out
3. <u>why</u>
4. dove

1. we'll
2. they'll
3. she'll
4. I'll

1. knees
2. blowing
3. yelling
4. between
5. agree

1. <u>coming</u>
2. <u>calling</u>
3. <u>having</u>
4. <u>standing</u>
5. <u>setting</u>

Waves scare me.

I hate to swim.

A Swim for Bob
Part Two

Bob and his pals were on the<u>ir</u> way to swim in the waves. Beth drove the van. Tim sat in back. He kept saying, "Why did I agree to go to the beach? Waves scare me."

Beth kept saying, "Yes, why did I agree to go? I hate to swim."

Bob kept saying, "But we will have lots of fun."

When the pals got to the beach, the wind was
blowing hard, and the waves were big. Bob dove into
the waves and swam like a seal. Tim went in the
waves up to his knees and then said, "This is not for
me."

Beth went in the waves, but she swam like a cat. She didn't like it. And she kept yelling to Bob, "Wait for me. Don't swim so fast."

But Bob didn't hear her. He was going over the waves, under the waves, and between the waves.

More to come.

ar oo ch al er ol

4

1. find
2. out
3. able
4. g<u>ir</u>l
5. get

1. <u>driving</u>
2. <u>diving</u>
3. <u>calling</u>
4. <u>coming</u>
5. <u>having</u>
6. <u>wasn</u>'t

1. week
2. m<u>all</u>
3. met
4. ten
5. ok<u>ay</u>

1. car<u>e</u>d
2. scared
3. s<u>oo</u>n
4. moon

11

It's time to go home.

A Swim for Bob
Part Three

Beth said, "I can't keep up with Bob." So after a while, she came from the waves and sat on the beach. Soon the sun started to go down. Beth began calling to Bob. "Bob, it's time to go home."

But Bob didn't hear her. He was diving and swimming and rolling and having so much fun that he didn't know it was time to leave.

At last, he went from the waves on to the beach. "Wasn't that fun?" he asked Beth.

"No," she said. "Now let's get Tim and go home."

But where was Tim? Beth and Bob went up and down the beach, but they didn't see Tim. They went to the van, but they didn't see him there. By now, the sun was down, and Bob was getting scared. He kept thinking, "I hope Tim is okay."

More to come.

1. yard
2. week
3. yes
4. ever
5. where

1. <u>sett</u>ing
2. <u>stand</u>ing
3. <u>try</u>ing
4. <u>some</u>body

1. find
2. saw
3. g<u>ir</u>l

1. sky
2. mall
3. met
4. zoo
5. room
6. ten

A Swim for Bob
Part Four

The sun was setting, and the m<u>oo</u>n was in the sky. Bob and Beth were trying to find Tim. They were standing next to the van. All at once, somebody said, "What time is it?"

Bob turned and saw Tim coming out of the van. Tim said, "I was sleeping in the back seat."

"Wow," Bob said. "Am I ever happy to see you."

Beth said, "Yes, I'm happy too. But we are late. Let's go home."

So the three pals got in the van and drove home.

Bob's dad met them as they drove up. Was Bob's dad happy? No.

Later that week, Beth and Tim went for a bike ride to the zoo. Did Bob go with them? No. He had to stay in his room.

Ten days later, Beth and Tim went to the mall. Did Bob go with them? No. He had to stay in his yard.

How many days do you think Bob will have to stay home?

The end.

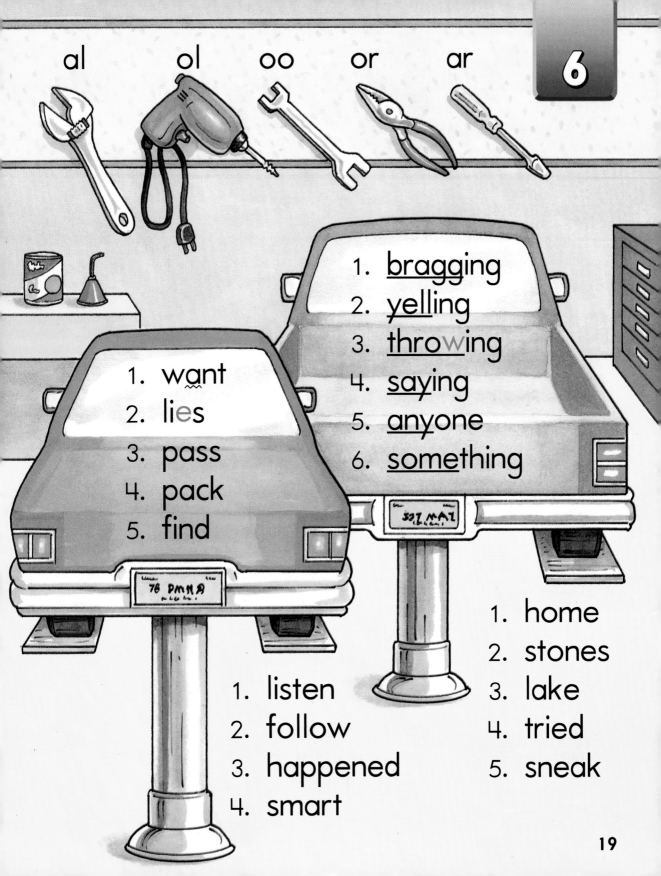

al   ol   oo   or   ar

6

1. <u>b</u>ragging
2. <u>y</u>elling
3. <u>throw</u>ing
4. <u>s</u>aying
5. <u>any</u>one
6. <u>some</u>thing

1. want
2. lies
3. pass
4. pack
5. find

1. home
2. stones
3. lake
4. tried
5. sneak

1. listen
2. follow
3. happened
4. smart

19

Tam Will Listen

Tam did not listen to her mom. Once, her mom said, "Follow me and stay on the path." Tam started to play with the stones near the path. Then she slipped and slid down the hill. Ow.

Later, her mom told Tam, "Do not go swimming in the deep part of the lake." But Tam swam in the deep part of the lake. She did not swim well, and she had to call for help.

But then something happened that made Tam start to listen. Her mom told her, "Do not let anyone in while I am at the store."

After her mom left, a man came by her home. He said, "I am here to fix your TV."

Tam was going to let him in, but she said to herself, "Every time I do not listen to my mom, something bad happens."

So she told the man, "You will have to come back another time."

The man went down the street and tried to sneak into a home. "That man is a robber," Tam said. She called the cops. They came and got the robber.

Later the cops told Tam, "You were very smart." And Tam's mom said, "And you listen very well."

The end.

oo   ar   al

1. else
2. m<u>oo</u>se
3. goose
4. live

1. <u>for</u>est
2. <u>fas</u>test
3. <u>kee</u>per
4. <u>swimm</u>er
5. <u>brag</u>ging

1. want
2. out
3. find
4. agreed

1. pack
2. meet
3. pass
4. lies

The Bragging Rats

A pack of rats lived on a farm. The<u>ir</u> home was not far from the pond.

There were two rats in the pack who made the other rats mad. These two rats did a lot of bragging and a lot of yelling at each other. They did not agree on which rat was the best at throwing, or which rat was the fastest at eating. These rats told a lot of lies. The other rats called them the bragging rats.

One time, the bragging rats did not agree on which rat was the fastest swimmer. One rat said, "I can swim so fast that I pass up seals and otters."

The other rat said, "I can swim so fast I don't get wet."

As the two rats were bragging, it started to rain. The bragging rats slipped into the pond. They were not able to get out. One rat said, "Help. This pond is too deep for me."

The other rats said, "We will help you get out, but you must stop saying how well you swim." The bragging rats agreed. After that, they never bragged about how well they swam. But they bragged about lots of other things.

The end.

u e i o a

1. <u>every</u>
2. <u>show</u>i<u>ng</u>
3. <u>we</u>'re
4. <u>they</u>'re

1. <u>rested</u>
2. <u>morning</u>
3. <u>setting</u>
4. <u>sitting</u>
5. <u>forest</u>
6. <u>keeper</u>

1. zoo
2. n<u>oo</u>n
3. down
4. town
5. met
6. meet

1. live
2. else
3. want
4. easy
5. fl<u>oa</u>t
6. swam

A Home in the Zoo
Part One

A goose and a m<u>oo</u>se were pals. They lived in a
f<u>or</u>est. Every day, they did the same thing. They
went to the pond. The m<u>oo</u>se went into the pond and
at<u>e</u> weeds while the goose swam. Then they got out
of the pond and sat in the grass. S<u>oo</u>n they went
back into the pond. At the end of the day, they went
home.

One day, the goose said to the m<u>oo</u>se, "I am getting sick of doing the same thing every day. We meet the same mol<u>e</u>s and the same birds. We go to the same pond. We need to do something else."

The m<u>oo</u>se said, "Why don't we go live in a zoo?"

The goose said, "That is a fine plan. Let's call a zoo and tell them that we plan to live there."

So the goose called the zoo and told the zoo keeper what they were thinking.

The zoo keeper said, "We have no room for another m<u>oo</u>se and another goose."

More to come.

1. want
2. wash
3. water

1. been
2. look
3. shiny
4. out
5. about
6. order

1. we're
2. trust
3. easy
4. noon
5. balloon
6. boom

1. morning
2. anybody
3. nobody
4. floating
5. sailing
6. showing

I can fly there.

Not me.

A Home in the Zoo
Part Two

After the goose called the zoo, the moose was very sad.

"I want to go to a zoo," he said. "Why can't we live in a zoo?"

The goose said, "You know, I can go to that zoo. All I need to do is fly there and land in the pond with other birds."

The moose said, "Yes, that's easy for you to do. But I can't fly. So how can I get there?"

The m<u>oo</u>se and the goose started to think, and
they kept thinking all m<u>or</u>ning. By n<u>oo</u>n they were still
thinking. Then the goose saw something in the pond.
It was a fl<u>o</u>ating leaf. And on that leaf were two little
bugs. They were sailing on that leaf.

The goose said, "Do you see those bugs on that leaf? They are showing us how to get to the zoo."

The moose asked, "Do you mean we are going to float on a leaf?"

"No," the goose said. "We will float there, but not on a leaf."

More to come.

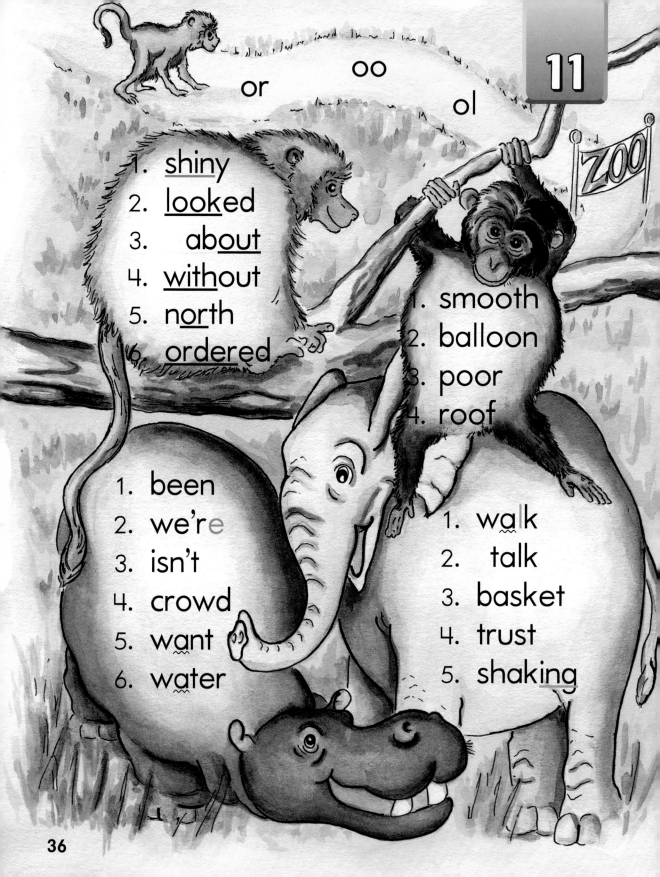

or

oo

ol

11

1. shiny
2. looked
3. about
4. without
5. north
6. ordered

1. smooth
2. balloon
3. poor
4. roof

1. been
2. we're
3. isn't
4. crowd
5. want
6. water

1. walk
2. talk
3. basket
4. trust
5. shaking

36

A Home in the Zoo
Part Three

The goose had told the moose that they were going to fl<u>oa</u>t to the zoo. The moose asked, "How can we fl<u>oa</u>t to the zoo?"

The goose said, "We will fl<u>oa</u>t in the sky. We will ride in a big balloon."

The moose l<u>oo</u>ked up in the sky and said, "Oh."

So the goose called a balloon shop and <u>or</u>dered a big balloon. But when the balloon came, the moose started to get cold feet. He said, "I don't know about this. I have never been flying before, and I am scar<u>e</u>d."

"Oh, come on," the goose said. "Flying is fun. Trust me. You will have fun in the sky."

The moose said, "I think I'm too scared to get in that balloon. What happens if it f<u>a</u>lls out of the sky?"

The goose said, "Well, I'll just fly away."

"And I'll f<u>a</u>ll down, like a rock," the moose said. "No thanks. I'll stay here."

More next time.

er   ar   or   ir

12

1. you'll
2. isn't
3. wonderful
4. folks

1. been
2. p<u>oo</u>r
3. r<u>oo</u>f
4. t<u>a</u>lking
5. walked
6. sm<u>oo</u>th

1. lions
2. tigers
3. apes
4. bab<u>oo</u>ns

1. <u>gather</u>ed
2. <u>be</u>low
3. <u>shaking</u>
4. <u>looking</u>
5. <u>without</u>

A Home in the Zoo
Part Four

The moose was scared. He didn't want to get into the balloon. The goose tried to talk the moose into going. "That balloon isn't going to fall out of the sky," he said. "And I won't go without you. The two of us will go, or the two of us will stay here. And I want to go."

The goose did lots and lots of talking that day. By the time the moon was coming up, the moose said, "Okay. I will go."

The next m<u>or</u>ning, the goose jumped into the basket of the balloon. "Let's go," he said to the moose. And the goose kept ta<u>l</u>king as the moose slowly got in the basket. That p<u>oo</u>r moose was shak<u>ing</u> with fear.

I want to go home.

Then the balloon started to go up and up. Soon it was way up in the sky.

The ride was very smooth, but the moose was still scared. He kept saying, "Why am I doing this? I want to go home."

The goose said, "We will soon be over the zoo."

More to come.

clock

ch sh h c

1. lion
2. baboon
3. tiger
4. ape

1. wonderful
2. gathered
3. believe
4. morning
5. nearly
6. forgot

1. north
2. everybody
3. below
4. inside
5. biggest

1. feather
2. baby
3. shiny
4. folks
5. air
6. crowds

I see the zoo below.

A Home in the Zoo
Part Five

It was nearly dark out. The m<u>oo</u>n was big and shiny. The goose said, "I see the zoo bel<u>ow</u>."

The moose said, "I want to go home."

The goose said, "I will try to land the balloon where the other moose live."

But just as the balloon was getting set to land on the r<u>oo</u>f of the moose home, a wind came up. The balloon went n<u>or</u>th. And when the balloon landed, the moose l<u>oo</u>ked out and said, "What is this? We are not in the moose home."

The next morning, lots of folks came to the zoo to see the lions and tigers. They came to see the birds and the apes. But the biggest crowds gathered near the baboon home.

The folks did not believe what they saw. Inside were 56 baboons, one hot air balloon, and one big moose. That moose had three baby baboons and one goose sitting on his back.

Everybody said, "What a wonderful show."

The end.

shark

1. <u>any</u>one
2. any<u>body</u>
3. <u>every</u>
4. vis<u>it</u>
5. <u>yell</u>ow
6. <u>forg</u>ot

1. <u>fea</u>thers
2. <u>t</u>ook
3. long
4. about
5. listened
6. many

1. nos<u>e</u>
2. bragged
3. shut
4. trick
5. f<u>oo</u>l
6. smarter

Who is Smarter?
Part One

One time the bragging rats yelled and bragged for a week. They were bragging about how smart they were. The rat with the big yellow teeth kept saying, "I am so smart that I know more things than anyone else."

The other bragging rat kept saying, "I forgot more things than you will ever know."

Those bragging rats told many lies. By the end of the week, the other rats were not able to stand it any more. So some of them went to the wise old rat. They asked him, "What can we do to stop the bragging rats from yelling all the time?"

The wise old rat said, "I think I have a plan that will keep them from talking for many days."

These feathers are part of my plan.

Later that day, the wise old rat went to visit the bragging rats. The wise old rat had two feathers. He told the other rats that these feathers were part of his plan to make the bragging rats stop talking.

What did the wise old rat plan to do with the feathers?

You will see next time.

boy   mail

1. ready
2. says
3. took
4. feather
5. stays

1. stand
2. started
3. smart
4. tricks
5. nose
6. fool

1. something
2. anything
3. anybody
4. forgot

1. longer
2. taking
3. smartest
4. listening
5. waved

Wait.

Who is Smarter?
Part Two

The wise old rat had a plan to make the bragging rats stop talking and yelling. He took two feathers with him. They were part of his plan.

When he came up to the bragging rats, the rat with yellow teeth was saying, "I am so smart that nobody can fool me or play tricks on me."

The other bragging rat started to say something, but the wise old rat said, "Wait. There is a way to see who is the smartest rat."

A smart rat can . . .

The bragging rats stopped yelling and listened. The wise old rat waved the feathers at the bragging rats and said, "A smart rat can stand so a feather stays on the end of his nose. If you can keep the feather on the end of your nose for a long time, you are very smart."

The rat with the yellow teeth said, "I can keep that feather on my nose for a week."

The rat with the long tail said, "I can do it way longer than that."

More next time.

socks   girl   rocks

1. <u>smart</u>er
2. smart<u>est</u>
3. <u>long</u>er
4. long<u>est</u>
5. <u>smil</u>ing

1. both
2. r<u>ea</u>dy
3. says
4. saw

1. lunch
2. sink
3. stays
4. dock
5. trick

1. <u>mis</u>ter
2. <u>winn</u>er
3. <u>any</u>body
4. <u>supp</u>er
5. <u>no</u>body

16

You see, it . . .

Who is Smarter?
Part Three

The wise old rat had a plan to keep the bragging rats from talking. He told them that the smarter rat can stand longer with a feather on his nose.

The wise old rat said, "Before you start, let me show you how hard it is to keep the feather from floating away." He set a feather on the end of his nose. Then he said, "You see, it . . . " As soon as he said "you," the feather went sailing into the air.

It is not easy.

Then the wise old rat said, "You see, it is not easy to keep the feather on your nose. But if you are very smart, you will think of a way to do it."

The rat with the yellow teeth said, "I know how to do it, but I'm not going to tell anybody else."

The rat with the long tail said, "I know how to do it too, and I can do it better and longer than you can."

"No you can't," the rat with yellow teeth said. "I'm the smartest rat, and I am ready to show you that I am."

This is not the end.

1. good
2. even
3. says
4. both

1. yet
2. still
3. clock
4. lunch
5. supper
6. hop

qu

1. smiling
2. small
3. winner
4. wanted
5. leader
6. mister

1. where
2. were
3. here
4. their

Who is Smarter?
Part Four

The bragging rats believe that the feathers show how smart they are.

The wise old rat set a clock near the bragging rats. Then he set a feather on the nose of each bragging rat. He said, "The clock will show us how long you can keep the feather on your nose."

Both the bragging rats were smiling, but they did not say a thing. They were thinking, "I know that I can't talk or the feather will float away."

The bragging rats were still all day long. The wise old rat let them take time out to eat lunch and supper. At the end of the day, he told them, "We do not have a winner. So you are both very smart."

"No," both the bragging rats said. "I am the smartest."

So they did the same thing the next day and the day after that. While each bragging rat was standing with a feather on his nose, the other rats were happy. They did not have to listen to lies and yelling. Every now and then, a rat walked by the bragging rats and said, "My, my. How smart you both are."

And each bragging rat smiled and said to himself, "Yes, I am so smart that nobody can trick me."

Everybody in the rat pack was happy.

The end.

cat   bells   boy   shells

qu

oo

oa

ch

sh

1. quick
2. queen
3. quit

1. wanted
2. wants
3. else
4. talked
5. good

1. Gorman
2. Joan
3. lead
4. toads
5. first
6. stream

1. because
2. somebody
3. needed
4. himself
5. funny
6. boating

Gorman and the Toads
Part One

Gorman did not see well. He wanted to go for a boat ride, but he needed somebody to lead him down to the lake. He asked all the other goats, "Who wants to go for a boat ride with me?"

Only one goat said, "I do. I do."

That goat was Joan. Gorman didn't want to go with her because she talked funny. She didn't say things one time. She said them two times. Anybody else says, "It's a fine day for boating."

Joan says, "It's a fine day for boating. It's a fine day for boating."

First, I have to . . .

Joan was the only goat who wanted to go boating with Gorman. So at last Gorman told Joan, "Okay. Let's go."

Joan said, "First, I have to ask my mother. First, I have to ask my mother."

Gorman said to himself, "This will not be a lot of fun. This will not be a lot of fun."

Joan ran home and talked to her mother. Then she came back and told Gorman, "My mother said I can't get wet. My mother said I can't get wet."

Gorman said, "How can you get wet? You will be in a safe boat."

More to come.

car   tree   star

ch

ck

qu

1. <u>qu</u>een
2. s<u>qu</u>eak
3. <u>qu</u>ick

1. <u>g</u>ood
2. stood
3. even
4. w<u>a</u>ter
5. how
6. who

1. dock
2. hope
3. seat
4. under
5. yet
6. s<u>oo</u>n

1. <u>leadi</u>ng
2. <u>talki</u>ng
3. <u>aski</u>ng
4. <u>mister</u>
5. <u>hopp</u>ed
6. <u>holds</u>

Gorman and the Toads
Part Two

Joan and Gorman were on their way to the lake. Joan was leading Gorman. She was also talking. Gorman was thinking, "This may not be a good plan."

Gorman and Joan walked and walked. Gorman kept asking, "Are we near the water yet?"

Joan kept saying, "Not yet. Not yet."

Get out.

At last Gorman and J<u>oa</u>n came to the dock where the boat was. Gorman said, "I will row. You can sit on the back seat."

J<u>oa</u>n said, "Oh, I hope I don't get wet. Oh, I hope I don't get wet."

Gorman said, "How can you get wet? Just sit on the back seat, and you won't get wet."

But just as Gorman was getting set to row the boat, somebody said, "Hold it. This is my home. Get out."

Joan jumped and said, "Who said that? Who said that?"

A big toad hopped from under the seat and said, "I said that. Now get out of my home."

Gorman said, "Who is talking?"

Joan said, "It's a toad. It's a toad."

Gorman said, "Well, Mister Toad, we are going for a boat ride, and you can't stop us."

More next time.

star   spoon   over

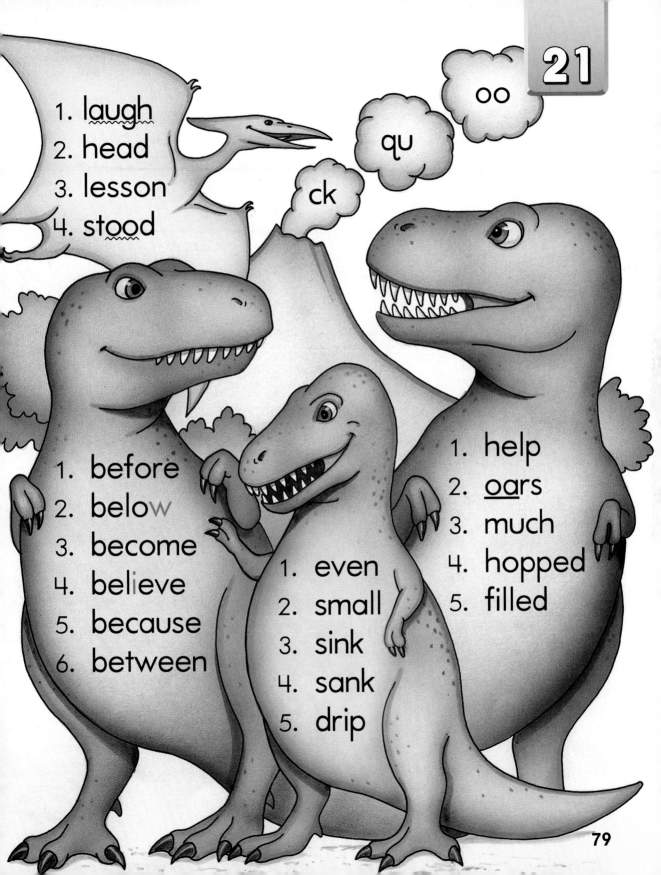

21

oo

qu

ck

1. laugh
2. head
3. lesson
4. stood

1. before
2. below
3. become
4. believe
5. because
6. between

1. even
2. small
3. sink
4. sank
5. drip

1. help
2. oars
3. much
4. hopped
5. filled

79

Leave now.

21

Gorman and the Toads
Part Three

A toad came out from below the back seat.
That toad told Gorman and Joan that the boat was
his home. He said, "Leave now, or you will soon be
in the water."

Gorman asked, "What do you mean?"

The toad said, "If you do not leave, I will sink
this boat."

Gorman said, "Ho, ho. You are much too small
to sink a boat."

"I have help," the toad said as he hopped up on the seat. "One call from me, and this boat will be filled with toads. They will sink the boat, and you will be in the water."

Joan said, "Oh, I can't go in the water. Oh, I can't go in the water."

Gorman said, "Don't even listen to that little toad. There is no way he can sink this boat."

The toad hopped to the front of the boat. He stood up on the front seat and said, "I will tell you once more. I am the leader toad. If I call for help, many toads will come. So leave this boat, now."

"No way," Gorman said.

More to come.

1. thank
2. sank
3. bank
4. slow
5. tow

1. Joan's
2. cheered
3. grabbed

1. hundred
2. head
3. laugh
4. oars
5. wade
6. brothers

1. quickly
2. landed
3. lower
4. leapers
5. creepers
6. ones

oo qu oa ol or

Gorman and the Toads
Part Four

The leader toad stood on the front seat and told Gorman and Joan, "I will sink this boat if you do not leave."

Gorman said, "Ho, ho. I don't think we have to listen to what this toad says."

Gorman grabbed the oars and started to row the boat away from the dock. The leader toad quickly jumped up on top of Joan's head and called out, "Brothers, sisters, and pals. Come home."

All at once, many, many toads started to leap
into the boat. They jumped from the dock. Some
of them hopped from trees. Some of them came
flying out of the water and landed in the boat. As
more and more toads landed in the boat, the boat
sank lower and lower and lower in the water.

Joan called out, "Oh no, I'm going to get wet. Oh no, I'm going to get wet." And she did.

First a little water came over the side of the boat. Then the boat filled up and sank quickly.

More next time.

rabbit

qu   ch   ck   wh

1. give
2. lesson
3. most
4. head
5. today
6. hundred

1. leapers
2. creepers
3. slipping
4. dripping

1. wad**ed**
2. laugh**ed**
3. cheer**ed**
4. stand**ing**
5. smil**ing**
6. sink**ing**

1. tow
2. bank
3. black
4. teach
5. blame
6. web

Gorman and the Toads
Part Five

There were almost a hundred toads in the water. There were little toads and big ones, brown ones, green ones, and black ones. Some were fat, and some were thin. Some were leapers, and some were creepers.

The toads were singing and swimming and laughing and having lots of fun. Many of them were yelling, "We did it. We sank that boat."

Gorman and Joan were in the water, but the water was not very deep. Joan kept saying, "Oh dear, what will Mother say? Oh dear, what will Mother say?"

The leader toad was standing on top of Joan's head. He was smiling and saying, "Thank you brothers. Thank you sisters. And thank you pals."

A big brown toad smiled and said, "When the leader toad says he will sink a boat, that boat will sink."

Another toad said, "Nobody is better at sinking boats than we are." The other toads cheered and laughed.

At last the leader toad told the other toads to tow the boat back to the bank of the lake. Gorman and Joan waded back and got out of the water. Joan was very wet.

This is not the end.

jump	fox

A snail did not like to smile or laugh. One day, she met a bug that was very happy. The bug said, "I can make you smile. I will rub a feather under your shell." That made the snail laugh.

1. Who did not smile very much?

2. Who told the snail that he could make her smile?

3. What did the bug rub under the snail's shell to make her laugh?

1. a<u>gain</u>
2. to<u>day</u>
3. spid<u>er</u>
4. a<u>bout</u>
5. less<u>on</u>

1. <u>g</u>ood
2. c<u>ou</u>ld
3. w<u>ou</u>ld
4. sh<u>ou</u>ld

1. live
2. give
3. jump
4. stump
5. game
6. blame

1. dripping
2. <u>or</u>dering
3. teaching
4. bit<u>ing</u>
5. smil<u>ing</u>

Gorman and the Toads
Part Six

Gorman and Joan were standing on the bank of the lake. The leader toad was <u>or</u>dering some other toads to bring the <u>oar</u>s to him. The toads were still singing and laughing. One little toad kept saying, "That was fun. Can we do it some more?"

Gorman and Joan were not having fun. They were dripping wet. Joan was saying, "I hope I dry fast. I hope I dry fast."

Everybody, listen up.

At last the leader toad yelled, "Everybody, listen up." The toads stopped talking and laughing.

The leader toad said to the other toads, "Give them their oars, and do it quickly."

Then the leader toad turned to Joan. He said, "Let that teach you a lesson. One toad is small, but many toads can sink boats. Now take your oars and get out of here. Tell your mother Gorman is to blame for getting you wet."

That's what Joan did. She told her mother that Gorman was to blame. She also told everybody else about Gorman and the toads.

Today, the goats still tell the story about the time the toads sank Gorman's boat.

The end.

cry

Two turtles took a trip to the beach. The turtles were sitting in the sun. A man was walking on the beach looking for stones. He said, "Here are two fine looking stones." And he picked up the turtles and took them home.

1. Who sat in the sun at the beach?

2. Who was picking up stones at the beach?

3. What did that man think the turtles were?

4. Where did the man take the turtles?

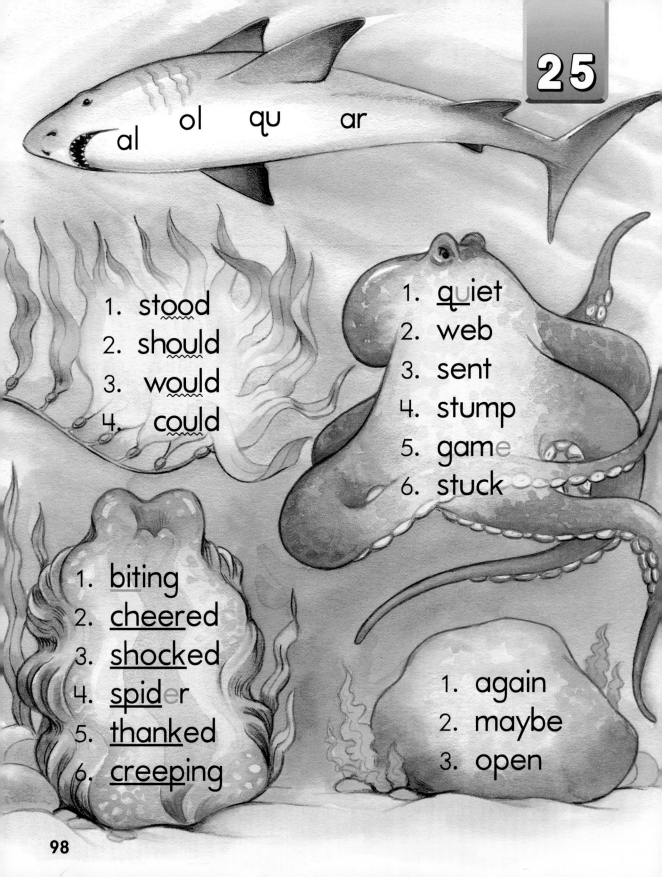

al   ol   qu   ar

1. stood
2. should
3. would
4. could

1. quiet
2. web
3. sent
4. stump
5. game
6. stuck

1. biting
2. cheered
3. shocked
4. spider
5. thanked
6. creeping

1. again
2. maybe
3. open

The Little Bug Bites
Part One

A little bug was the best biting bug, but he didn't bite a lot. His mom told him that good bugs didn't bite if they didn't have to.

One time, he did have to bite. He was playing with Jill, her brother, and her sister. They were on a stump, playing a game of jump.

"I can jump far," Jill said. And she jumped from one side of the stump to the other side.

Jill's brother said, "I can do better than that."
He jumped from one side of the stump and sailed
over the other side. The other bugs cheered. But
when they saw where he landed, they were
shocked. He was in a spider web.

"Help, help," he called. "I'm stuck in this
web."

A big spider was not far away, and that spider
was starting to come after Jill's brother.

"Help," her brother called again. The spider
was creeping closer to Jill's brother. Jill's brother
was scared, and so were the other bugs.

Jill said, "What can we do?"

More next time.

drink

An old farmer had socks that smelled bad. He said, "I think my socks stink. So I will wash them in the sink." He did that. Now he says, "My socks smell good, just like they should."

1. What smelled bad?

2. Where did the farmer wash them?

3. How do they smell now?

1. wa<u>tch</u>
2. w<u>a</u>sh
3. spid<u>e</u>r
4. sh<u>ou</u>ld
5. l<u>oo</u>ked
6. w<u>ou</u>ld

1. web
2. open
3. sent
4. steep

1. <u>trail</u>
2. <u>creep</u>ing
3. <u>hiker</u>
4. <u>line</u>d
5. <u>go</u>es

1. roar<u>ed</u>
2. start<u>s</u>
3. plan<u>s</u>
4. blam<u>ed</u>
5. sav<u>ing</u>
6. bit<u>er</u>

The Little Bug Bites
Part Two

Jill's brother was stuck in a spider web. The spider was creeping closer and closer to Jill's brother. He was scared. So were the others. "What can we do?" Jill asked.

The little bug said, "We can do some big time biting." The little bug jumped down into the web and started to bite a hole in the web. Then he told Jill's brother, "Jump down into this hole, and you will be safe."

Roarrrr.

But the spider was now very close, and it looked very mean. The little bug looked at the spider and said, "Stay back, or I will take a big bite out of you."

The spider smiled and said, "You make me laugh. Show me your best bite."

The little bug showed his teeth and said, "This is how my bite starts out. Then I open wide and roar like this." The bug opened up so wide and made such a big roar that it almost sent the spider flying.

That spider ran and hid while the little bug and Jill's brother got out of the web.

After the bugs were safe, Jill gave the little bug a big hug. Then she told him, "You are such a good biter. Thank you for saving my brother."

The end.

A man grabbed two stones at the beach and took them home. Those stones were really turtles. When the man got home, he set the turtles in his yard.

When he came back, he said, "My stones are walking back to the beach."

The man chased after the turtles.

1. What did a man think he grabbed at the beach?

2. What did the man really grab?

3. Where did the man set them?

4. Where did the turtles go?

1. watch<u>ed</u>
2. happen<u>ed</u>
3. blam<u>ed</u>
4. go<u>es</u>
5. dirt<u>y</u>
6. stay<u>s</u>

1. steep
2. slip
3. kept
4. sneeze
5. slide
6. line

1. mak<u>ing</u>
2. jok<u>ing</u>
3. walking
4. talking
5. telling
6. cleaning

The Big Goat Hike
Part One

Nine goats made plans to go on a hike. They were going to follow a trail over five hills.

Joan was one of the goats who planned to go on this hike. Gorman also planned to go. But Joan's mom did not like that part of the plan.

She did not want Joan to get wet or to get dirty. She blamed Gorman for what happened the last time Joan went with him. So she told the other goats, "If Gorman goes, Joan stays home. If Gorman goes, Joan stays home."

Joan did not want to stay home. She kept telling her mom that she would not walk near Gorman. She said that no goats would go near the pond. She told her mom, "We will be in the hills. We will be in the hills."

But her mom kept telling Joan, "No, you can't go. No, you can't go."

For days, Joan and her mother talked and talked. The more they talked, the more the other goats made jokes about Gorman and the toads.

More to come.

skate	27

Ann's mom told Ann and her pals to p<u>ai</u>nt the dock green. So the g<u>ir</u>ls got a p<u>ai</u>l of p<u>ai</u>nt and began to p<u>ai</u>nt. Ann's brother was out boating. So he didn't have to help p<u>ai</u>nt.

1. Who p<u>ai</u>nted the dock?

2. They p<u>ai</u>nted the dock so it was ▮▮▮▮.

3. Did Ann's brother help p<u>ai</u>nt?

4. Her brother was out ▮▮▮▮.

1. pla<u>ce</u>
2. w<u>ou</u>ld
3. sh<u>ou</u>ld
4. c<u>ou</u>ld

1. <u>wash</u>ed
2. <u>hike</u>r
3. <u>every</u>body
4. <u>no</u>body

1. steep
2. strike
3. lead
4. led
5. agree
6. until

1. jok<u>ing</u>
2. dirty
3. funny
4. mak<u>ing</u>
5. asking
6. lined

113

The Big Goat Hike
Part Two

Joan and her mom talked and talked about the hike in the hills. While they talked, the other goats kept making jokes about Gorman. One goat kept asking, "Gorman, if you go on this hike, should I take my swim things with me?"

Another goat kept saying, "If I go on this hike, will I end up with a toad on my head?"

Oh, how the goats laughed and laughed at these jokes. But Gorman did not think they were very funny.

On the day before the hike, the goats were in the barn making jokes about Gorman and the toads. They stopped joking when they saw Joan and her mother walking over to the barn.

Joan's mother looked very mad. She told the goats, "Joan really wants to go. Joan really wants to go." She told the goats that Joan could not get dirty. Then she told Gorman, "If Joan gets dirty, I will blame you. If Joan gets dirty, I will blame you."

Gorman said, "Well, I . . . I don't know what to say . . . I . . . " Joan and her mother and the goats talked and talked. At last, everybody agreed. Joan would go on the hike, and Gorman would go, too. Nobody would go near water or mud. And Gorman would never lead the way.

More next time.

cow   white   black   hay

Three apes said, "Let's go fishing." So they went on a little train to the lake. Then they walked to the fishing hole. Did they come home with a lot of fish? No, they forgot to bring their fishing poles with them.

1. Who went fishing?

2. What did they ride on?

3. Did they get lots of fish?

4. They forgot to bring their ███████.

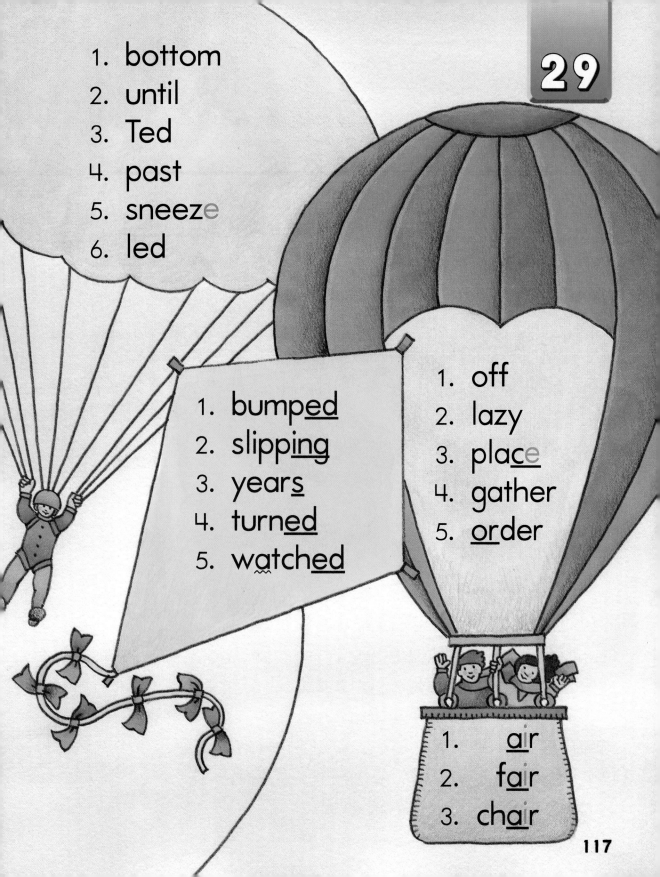

1. bottom
2. until
3. Ted
4. past
5. sneeze
6. led

1. bumped
2. slipping
3. years
4. turned
5. watched

1. off
2. lazy
3. place
4. gather
5. order

1. air
2. fair
3. chair

The Big Goat Hike
Part Three

The goats were ready for the hike. Joan could go with them, but the goats could not go near water and mud. And Gorman would never lead. He would have to stay at the end of the line.

The nine goats lined up. The first goat was named Ted. He was a good hill hiker. So he was the leader. Gorman was the last goat in line. Joan was just in front of him.

We'll have to take the old trail.

The goats followed the trail over three hills.
Then they came to a hive of mean bees. Ted said,
"We can't go on this trail. We'll have to take the
old trail that is next to the lake."

So Ted led the way to the old trail. This trail was very steep, and it went up and up, next to the lake.

When the goats almost got to the top of the hill, they came to a pla<u>ce</u> where the trail stopped. The trail was washed out. Ted told the other goats, "We'll have to go back."

So each goat slowly turned to go back down the trail. Now Ted was not the leader. Ted was at the back end of the line. Who was the leader now? Gorman, that's who.

More to come.

snake   eggs

Last summer, Pam bragged to her pals, "I will swim with the otters." They said, "You won't be able to do that." But she did that. She told everybody what she did and how much fun it was. Pam's pals are sick of listening to her.

1. Who did Pam swim with?

2. Who did she tell about it?

3. Did her pals like to listen to Pam?

1. stories
2. couldn't
3. washing
4. bath
5. pass

1. lazy
2. off
3. again
4. bottom
5. bump
6. past

1. because
2. before
3. began
4. between

1. sliding
2. rolling
3. standing
4. grabbing
5. cleaning

The Big Goat Hike
Part Four

The goats had to turn back because the trail was washed out. So now Gorman was the first goat in line.

Joan said, "But Gorman can't lead. But Gorman can't lead."

The other goats told Joan that she would have to be the leader. She would have to go past Gorman. But there was not much room.

Joan told Gorman, "Stand still, and I will pass you. Stand still, and I will pass you."

She started to pass Gorman, but just then, Gorman had to sneeze. He said, "I think I am going . . . to . . . " And he sneezed so hard that he bumped Joan.

She started to slide. So she grabbed on to Gorman and said, "Help, I am slipping. Help, I am slipping."

Both Joan and Gorman slid from the path all the way to the bottom of the hill. There was deep mud at the bottom of the hill. Joan and Gorman slid into that mud and rolled over and over. They looked like mud balls.

I didn't want to be leader.

The other goats did not want to laugh, but they could not help it. As they watched Gorman and Joan sitting in the mud, they laughed so hard that one of them slid off the path and landed in the mud, too.

This is not the end.

Two bugs liked the m<u>oo</u>n. One of them said, "I'm going to fly to the m<u>oo</u>n."

The other bug said, "Me too."

So those bugs started to fly to the m<u>oo</u>n. Then a big balloon came by and went in front of the m<u>oo</u>n.

One bug said, "I do not see the m<u>oo</u>n. I think the m<u>oo</u>n went home."

The other bug said, "Then we sh<u>ou</u>ld go home too." And they did.

1. What did the bugs w<u>a</u>nt to fly to?

2. What went in front of the m<u>oo</u>n?

3. One bug said that the m<u>oo</u>n went ▬▬▬.

4. Where did the bugs go?

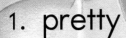

1. pretty
2. seconds
3. ch<u>ai</u>rs
4. dry
5. stories
6. until

1. look
2. cook
3. c<u>ou</u>ldn't
4. washing

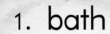

1. bath
2. landing
3. strik<u>e</u>
4. slid<u>ing</u>
5. tak<u>ing</u>
6. sneez<u>e</u>

1. serve
2. shap<u>e</u>
3. third
4. cry
5. sack

The Big Goat Hike
Part Five

The goats had a good laugh over Joan and Gorman sliding down the hill and landing in a pool of mud. As the goats walked home, the mud on Joan, Gorman, and the other goat started to dry. Soon these goats looked like they were tan dirt cakes.

The other goats laughed and laughed. But when they saw who was waiting at the barn, they stopped laughing. It was Joan's mother.

When Joan saw her mother, she yelled, "Mom, look what happened. Mom, look what happened."

Joan's mother took one look at Joan and said, "Who . . . what? Who . . . what?" Then she looked at the goat next to Gorman and said, "You did this. You did this."

Gorman said, "I had to sneeze. I couldn't help it."
Joan said, "I need a bath. I need a bath."
Her mother said, "Oh, how I hate dirt. Oh, how I hate dirt."

So Joan and her mother left to give Joan a bath. As soon as they were out of the barn, the other goats started to laugh again. But Gorman didn't laugh. He kept saying, "I had to sneeze. I couldn't help it."

After that day, the goats told two stories about Gorman. One was about the time the toads sank his boat. The other was about the time he sneezed on the path.

The end.

dropped

Debby's tractor didn't run very well. So she took her tractor to Tom's shop. Tom didn't know how to fix the tractor. So Debby traded the tractor for three bikes. She has one big bike and two little ones. She has more fun with her bikes than she did with her tractor.

1. What didn't run very well?

2. Where did Debby take the tractor?

3. Did Tom know how to fix it?

4. She traded her tractor for ▆▆▆▆.

qu   z   x   ol   or

1. c<u>oo</u>l
2. pool
3. c<u>oo</u>k
4. took
5. spring
6. bring

1. Homer
2. strik<u>e</u>
3. pl<u>ai</u>n
4. f<u>ai</u>r
5. liv<u>e</u>s

1. <u>within</u>
2. <u>them</u>selves
3. <u>any</u>thing
4. <u>my</u>self
5. <u>your</u>self

1. wash<u>ing</u>
2. look<u>ing</u>
3. year<u>s</u>
4. hang<u>ing</u>

The Big Strike
Part One

There were big ants and little ants in an ant hill. For years and years, the big ants gave orders to the little ants. For years and years, the little ants did what the big ants told them to do. If a big ant told little ants to gather seeds, the little ants would gather seeds. If a big ant said, "Drive me to the lake," the little ants would do that. They would get in the ant van and drive the big ant to the lake.

The little ants did all the washing and all the cleaning and all the other things that had to be done to keep the ant hill looking good.

As the years went by, the big ants gave more and more orders to the little ants. The little ants started to feel that the big ants were just lazy and mean. But the little ants didn't say anything until one spring day. On that day, a little ant named Homer said, "I just took my last order from those big lazy ants."

A big ant had just ordered the little ants to bring a load of chairs to the swimming pool. "Not me," Homer said. "I'm going on strike."

More next time.

brown   ball

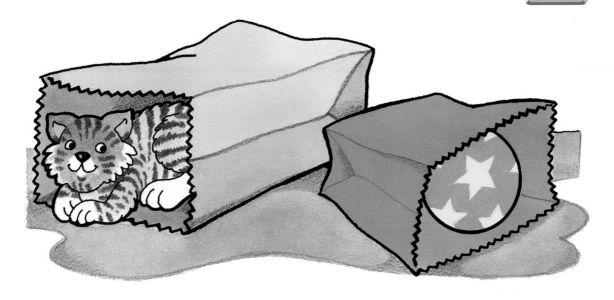

   Ann's mom had a van. One day, she loaded many things inside the van. She loaded some things on the r<u>oo</u>f. She even loaded some things on the back of the van. Then she said, "Now there is no room for me in this van."

1. Who had a van?

2. Did she load many things into the van?

3. After she loaded the van, what was there no room for in the van?

aw qu ck aw al

1. <u>aw</u>ful
2. <u>law</u>n
3. h<u>awk</u>

1. long
2. song
3. sang
4. hang

1. these
2. r<u>oo</u>f
3. quick
4. <u>qu</u>iet
5. within
6. does

1. making
2. taking
3. talking
4. walking

1. racket
2. care
3. themselves
4. seconds

The Big Strike
Part Two

Homer had told the other little ants that he was going on strike.

The other little ants asked, "What does that mean, going on strike?"

Homer said, "When you go on strike, you stop doing the things those big ants tell you to do. I think we should all go on strike and let those big ants start taking care of themselves."

The little ants looked at each other, and then some of them said, "Yes, let's go on strike."

Soon the other little ants agreed. "Yes, we little ants are going on strike."

One very little ant said, "But now that we are on strike, what will we do?"

Homer said, "Well, we can do anything we want to do."

Somebody asked, "Do you mean we can go swimming?"

"Why not?" Homer said.

Somebody else asked, "Do you mean we can just take the van for a drive?"

"Yes," Homer said. "And I think we should do that now."

Within three seconds, the van was filled with little ants. There were also ants on the roof and ants hanging all over the van. They laughed and sang as Homer drove the van down the road.

More to come.

A girl wanted to make a cake for Mother's Day. The girl asked her older sister to show her how to make a cake. Her sister said, "I'll show you the best way I know."

She and her sister gathered their cash. They went to a store and came home with a wonderful cake. It made their mother very happy.

1. Who did the girl ask about making a cake?

2. Did her sister have a plan?

3. Where did the girls go?

4. Did they make a cake or get one at a store?

qu   oa   aw

1. awful
2. hawk
3. yawn
4. draw

1. scrape
2. shape
3. done
4. won

1. live
2. live
3. pretty
4. fair

1. ourselves
2. themselves
3. complain
4. yourself
5. myself

1. field
2. racket
3. watched
4. does

I'm going to eat seeds.

The Big Strike
Part Three

As Homer drove the van, the other little ants were making an <u>aw</u>ful racket. They were yelling and singing and telling jok<u>e</u>s. At last, Homer drove into a field and stopped.

"What are we going to do here?" some of the ants asked.

Homer said, "I'm going to gather some seeds and eat them myself."

The little ants had never done anything like that
before. At first, they just stood and watched as
Homer ate seeds. Pretty soon, other little ants started
doing what Homer was doing. One of the very little
ants gathered a big pile of seeds and ate all of them.
Then he looked at Homer and said, "Burp."

Just then, ten big ants came up the road. They were not in good shape. They had never walked so far in their lives. Their leader was named Hawk because he looked like a hawk. He said, "You little ants can't strike. It's not fair."

Homer said, "It seems fair to me. We're having a good time."

Hawk said, "The strike is not fair. If you are on strike, who will take care of us?"

Homer said, "You will have to take care of yourself."

One big ant said, "But we don't know how to do that."

More next time.

A fox tried to trick Dan. Dan was eating an ear of corn. The fox told Dan, "Go in back of the tree, and I will show you a funny trick."

Dan went in back of the tree. The fox picked up the corn and started to run away with it. The fox tripped and fell into a mole hole. Dan laughed and said, "That is a very funny trick."

1. Who tried to trick somebody?

2. Who did the fox try to trick?

3. What was the fox trying to steal from Dan?

4. Did the fox get away with the corn?

149

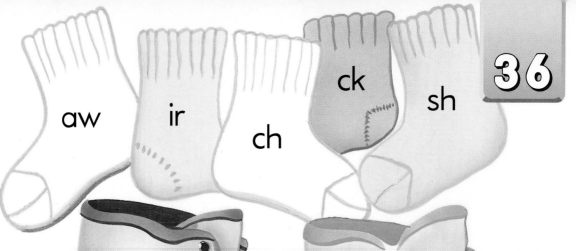

aw ir ch ck sh

1. l<u>ou</u>d
2. sh<u>ou</u>t
3. h<u>ou</u>se
4. <u>ou</u>r

1. s<u>er</u>ve
2. <u>qu</u>it
3. dr<u>aw</u>
4. l<u>aw</u>n
5. sa<u>ck</u>

1. room
2. took
3. tired
4. piled
5. been

1. <u>c</u>omplaining
2. <u>listening</u>
3. <u>ou</u>rselves
4. <u>cr</u>ying

1. work
2. w<u>ai</u>l
3. hungry
4. rest

The Big Strike
Part Four

The big ants did not want the little ants to strike. The big ants kept saying, "Who will keep the ant hill clean? Who will take us to the pool? Who will do all the awful things that must be done?"

Homer said, "I don't know who will do all those things, but we won't, because we are on strike."

Another little ant said, "I feel like going for a swim."

Other ants agreed. So the little ants piled into the ant van and drove to the pool. For a long time, they dove and swam and played water games. This was the first time they had ever been in the pool. Only big ants went in the pool before the strike.

After the little ants were tired of swimming, they took a nap on the lawn near the pool.

While the little ants were sleeping, the big ants gathered back at the ant hill. One of them said, "Who is going to take us swimming?"

Another ant said, "Who is going to s<u>er</u>ve me something to eat?"

Another ant said, "And who is going to clean up my room?"

At last H<u>a</u>wk said, "Stop compl<u>ai</u>ning. We must take car<u>e</u> of <u>ou</u>rselves."

The other big ants did not say anything for a long time.

More next time.

A little mole liked to dig holes. She dug too many holes. At last her mom told her, "Don't dig so many holes ar<u>ou</u>nd here. Go on the other side of the hill and dig there."

The little mole did that. Later that day, the little mole came back with a big lump of gold. Now all the moles dig on the other side of the hill.

1. What did the little mole like to do?

2. Who told her to dig some where else?

3. Did the mole dig on the other side of the hill?

4. What did the little mole find?

ou

or

oa

ou

ol

1. our
2. found
3. proud
4. round
5. around

1. <u>wailing</u>
2. <u>cry</u>ing
3. <u>howl</u>ing
4. <u>lasted</u>
5. <u>shout</u>ed

1. hungry
2. work
3. workers
4. rest
5. ti<u>r</u>ed
6. th<u>ir</u>d

1. <u>to</u>gether
2. <u>chores</u>
3. <u>sacks</u>
4. <u>picked</u>

The Big Strike
Part Five

Hawk told the big ants that they had to take
care of themselves. But at first, the big ants just
kept on compl<u>ai</u>ning. They said, "We can't do
h<u>a</u>rd work. We are not worker ants. We need
somebody to s<u>er</u>ve us."

By the th<u>ir</u>d day, the ants were crying and w<u>ai</u>ling.
"I'm hungry," they sh<u>ou</u>ted. "I need f<u>oo</u>d."

156

By the third day, Hawk was getting tired of listening to the big ants cry and wail. He said, "You can stay here and complain. I'm going to the field and gather seeds."

"Oh good," one of the other ants said. "Bring some seeds back for me."

"No," Hawk said. "I will eat the seeds that I gather."

"But how will the rest of us get seeds?" the ant asked.

And Hawk told him.

Hawk took a sack and hiked to the field. Some of the other big ants went with him and picked seeds. After they filled the sack, they sat down and ate. One of the ants said, "This work is not too hard."

Another ant said, "You know, I think I like gathering seeds."

Another ant turned to Hawk, smiled, and said, "Burp."

This is not the end.

goat   sleep

A big red butterfly lived near a farm. One day the farmer saw the butterfly and said, "I want that butterfly." The farmer got a net and went after the butterfly. The butterfly landed on top of a bee hive. The farmer took his net and tried to trap the butterfly, but the butterfly got away. And the net hit the bee hive. That did not make the bees happy. They chased the farmer back to the farm.

1. Who wanted to get the butterfly?

2. Was the butterfly red, yellow, or green?

3. The butterfly landed on a ▮▮▮▮.

4. Who chased the farmer back to the farm?

or   ou   qu

38

1. f<u>ou</u>nd
2. bell
3. felt
4. shy
5. ch<u>o</u>res

1. f<u>our</u>th
2. ar<u>ou</u>nd
3. be<u>ing</u>
4. <u>to</u>gether

1. h<u>oo</u>ves
2. foot
3. g<u>oo</u>d
4. speed
5. sheep
6. sleek

1. ranger
2. blanket
3. problem
4. h<u>or</u>se
5. pr<u>ou</u>d

160

The Big Strike
Part Six

By noon on the third day of the strike, most of the big ants were working. A lot of them gathered seeds. Three of them drove the ant van. They were not very good drivers, but they agreed, "This is a lot of fun."

Some big ants even started cleaning up the ant hill.

By noon on the fourth day, all of the big ants were working, and they were pretty proud of themselves.

The next day was the last day of the strike. That day the big ants got up and did all the ch<u>or</u>es that the little ants had done for them. One of the big ants said, "You know, we were pretty mean to those little ants. We didn't even say thank you."

Near the end of the last day, Hawk and 20 other big ants went to where the little ants were playing.

The big ants said, "We f<u>ou</u>nd out that we don't hate h<u>a</u>rd work."

Homer said, "And we f<u>ou</u>nd out that it is not fun to be lazy all the time."

So the ants agreed to end the strike. Today, big ants are not ordering little ants ar<u>ou</u>nd. All the ants work together, and when the work is over, all the ants play together.

This is the end.

leaf   bone

A farmer had sweet butter. He said, "Sweet butter makes better batter. That batter is never bitter." The farmer started to make batter for buns.

When he was not looking, the brown fox came over and took the sweet butter. That fox left his bitter butter. The farmer made batter with that butter. Later, the farmer tasted the buns he had made. He said, "Yuk. Those buns are bitter."

1. Who was going to bake something?

2. What was he going to bake?

3. Did he start out with sweet butter or bitter butter?

4. Who left the bitter butter for the farmer?

5. How did the buns taste?

1. knew
2. heard
3. high
4. higher
5. buck
6. wasted

1. sharp
2. pound
3. horse
4. stream

1. Agnes
2. foot
3. ranger
4. blanket
5. sleek
6. hooves

1. he'll
2. shy
3. running
4. bell
5. sees
6. speed

A Horse Named Agnes
Part One

Agnes was a very shy horse who lived on the farm with Gorman and Joan.

Agnes was not a pretty horse, but she was pretty big. She had hooves that were so big that she could not keep up with the other horses when they ran fast. She tried, but her hooves were not good for fast running.

Agnes really liked a <u>ho</u>rse named Al, but he didn't like her. He called her Big F<u>oo</u>t. Every morning, he went out with a little <u>ho</u>rse named Bell. They ran and jumped and ran some more.

I just saw the ranger near the road.

Al liked to show off his speed because the ranger was looking for a horse. Every morning, Al would ask Agnes, "Do I look sleek today? Is my tail pretty? Do I look too fat?" She would tell him that he looked fine. Then he would go out with Bell and show off. He kept telling Agnes, "One of these days, the ranger is going to come around here. When he sees me, he'll know that I am the horse for him."

Al kept showing off day after day, but the ranger didn't show up. Then one day, Gorman told a cow that he saw the ranger near the farm. What he really saw was a blanket hanging over a mail box. But the cow didn't know that.

More to come.

road fox grass

Mark got a job in a shop that sold f<u>oo</u>d. The g<u>ir</u>l who gave Mark the job told him, "The faster you do things, the more cash we make."

So Mark did things very fast. Mark set tables very quickly. He cleaned tables as fast as he set them. He cooked f<u>oo</u>d quickly. But when the folks who ordered the f<u>oo</u>d tasted it, they said, "Yuk."

Now Mark doesn't cook quickly, and everybody likes the f<u>oo</u>d they order.

1. Where did Mark get a job?

2. Mark set tables and cleaned tables ▬▬▬▬.

3. Did folks like Mark's f<u>oo</u>d when he cooked it quickly?

4. Do folks like the f<u>oo</u>d Mark makes now?

1. sleek
2. sheep
3. higher
4. sharp
5. turns
6. buck

1. behind
2. alone
3. heard
4. knew
5. less
6. plop

1. farther
2. wished
3. pounding
4. flowing
5. wasted
6. streams

A H<u>or</u>se Named Agnes
Part Two

Gorman told a cow that the ranger was near the farm. The cow told a h<u>or</u>se, and that h<u>or</u>se told all the other h<u>or</u>ses. So almost all the h<u>or</u>ses went out to show off. But before the h<u>or</u>ses left the barn, they asked Agnes things like, "How do I look? Is my coat sm<u>oo</u>th and sleek? Does my tail look good?"

Agnes told the other horses that they looked fine. And then they quickly ran from the barn and up to higher hills where they could be seen for miles.

Poor Agnes would watch them from the barn. She would watch them leap, and chase each other, and make sharp turns, and kick, and buck. And she would think, "Why can't I be quick and sleek like those horses?" She wished her hooves would get smaller so that Al would like her more.

The ranger didn't show up that day. And later
the horses did a lot of complaining because they
wasted a lot of time showing off.

About a week later, the horses heard once
more that the ranger was coming to the farm.
Two sheep had heard the farmer talking about the
ranger's visit. The sheep told a cow. She told a
horse, and soon all the horses knew about the
visit.

When Al found out that the ranger was coming,
he told Agnes, "Follow me around. You won't be
able to keep up, but try to stay close."

More next time.

The <u>qu</u>een of the toads was the best reader in the pond. All the other toads came to hear her read. After she was done reading a sh<u>or</u>t story, the toads clapped a little bit. After she was done reading a longer story, the toads clapped more. Did the toads clap even more after she was done reading a very long story? No. Most of the toads fell asleep.

1. Who was the best reader in the pond?

2. What did the other toads do after she was done reading a sh<u>or</u>t story?

3. When she was done reading a longer story, the toads clapped ▮▮▮▮▮.

4. Why didn't the toads clap when she was done reading a very long story?

1. <u>sticky</u>
2. a<u>lone</u>
3. <u>fa</u>rther
4. <u>pounding</u>
5. <u>flow</u>ing
6. <u>floa</u>ted

1. truck
2. felt
3. fell
4. less
5. plop
6. streams

1. d<u>oor</u>
2. behind
3. knew
4. second
5. problem
6. <u>aw</u>ful

1. step
2. paths
3. fields
4. turning

Next to you, I look ten times better.

A Horse Named Agnes
Part Three

Al wanted to show off for the ranger, so he told Agnes to stay as close to him as she could.

"I'll try," she said, and she felt very good because Al wanted her around.

But then Al told her why he wanted her near him. "I look wonderful when I'm standing alone," he said. "But when I'm standing next to you, I look ten times better. The ranger will pick me in a second."

"Oh," Agnes said, and she felt very sad.

On the morning that the ranger was coming to the farm, Al and little Bell were the first ones out of the barn. Al called to Agnes as they left, "Come on, Big Foot, try to keep up." And away they went. But they went so fast that Agnes could not stay with them. She fell farther and farther behind, and soon she could not see Al and Bell.

So Agnes started walking back to the barn. And just then, an awful rain storm began. In less than ten seconds, the rain was pounding down so hard that most of the horses started running back to the barn.

Before long, streams of water were flowing down the hills. The fields were turning into lakes. And the paths were turning into a sea of mud.

The other horses were slipping and sliding in the mud. But the mud was no problem for Agnes. Her hooves were so big that they almost floated on the mud. She just walked back to the barn without slipping once—plop, plop, plop.

This is not the end.

cleaned   clock   pants

The queen of the toads was a good hopper. But she could read much better than she could hop. A lot of the other toads were good hoppers, but they could not read very well. The queen told them that she would teach them how to read better. And she did. Now there are a lot of toads that read better than they hop. In fact, some of those toads can read better than the queen.

1. Who said she would teach other toads how to read?

2. At first, some toads could hop better than they could ▮▮▮▮▮.

3. Now a lot of toads read better than they can ▮▮▮▮▮.

4. Do any toads read better than the queen?

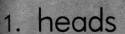

1. heads
2. y rds
3. steps
4. cheers

1. d<u>oor</u>
2. floor
3. stuck
4. truck
5. took
6. shook

1. <u>some</u>where
2. <u>any</u>how
3. <u>missing</u>
4. <u>muddy</u>
5. <u>sticky</u>

1. ti<u>e</u>
2. str<u>ai</u>n
3. nodded
4. blush<u>ed</u>

183

A Horse Named Agnes
Part Four

The rain and mud were <u>aw</u>ful. Almost all of the horses made it back to the barn. But two were missing. Al and Bell were still out there somewhere.

At last, the horse standing next to Agnes said, "I'm going to find them."

She ran out of the barn and started up the path. But before she went ten yards, she was stuck in the mud. It took her a long time to make her way back to the barn. She said, "No horse can go in that mud. It's too deep and sticky."

A little while later, one of the horses said, "Look, look. There's the ranger's truck." It was hard to see it in the rain, but there it was, near the farm h<u>ou</u>se. It was stuck in the mud. The d<u>oor</u> was open, and the ranger was getting out. But after he took three steps, he was stuck in the mud.

All the horses in the barn agreed that they had to do something to help the ranger. But what could they do? One horse said, "We'll just get stuck if we go out there."

Agnes said, "Well, I think I can go out there without getting stuck."

"No you can't," the other horses said. "That mud is too deep and sticky."

Agnes said, "Well, I think I'll try anyhow."

More next time.

worm   green   grass

Kim and Dan took their bikes to the beach. Kim said, "I won't ride close to the waves because I don't want to get wet."

Dan said, "Ho, ho. I'm going to ride near the waves. I won't get wet."

So they went down to the beach on their bikes. One of them got very wet. The other one said, "You got too close to the waves."

1. Who took their bikes to the beach?

2. Who did not want to ride near the waves?

3. Who wanted to ride near the waves?

4. Did Dan think he would get wet?

5. Who got wet?

1. tied
2. dried
3. long
4. strong

1. straining
2. cheers
3. blushed
4. heads
5. nodded
6. muddy

1. eyes
2. buy
3. shook
4. hip hip hooray
5. ashamed

1. he will ⟶ he'll
2. she is ⟶ she's
3. they are ⟶ they're
4. I would ⟶ I'd
5. she would ⟶ she'd

How does she do that?

plop, plop

A Horse Named Agnes
Part Five

Agnes walked over to the ranger without sinking into the mud one time. The ranger got on her back, and Agnes walked back to the barn, plop, plop, plop. The other horses were shocked. They were saying things like, "Did you see that? I don't know how she does that."

The ranger got off and looked ar<u>ou</u>nd the barn. Then he said, "Where is Al? He's one of the horses I've come to see." The horses shook their heads to tell the ranger that Al was not ar<u>ou</u>nd.

The ranger said, "Do any of you horses know where he is?" Agnes nodded her head up and down.

The ranger grabbed some rope and said, "Well, let's find him." He got on Agnes. She walked from the barn, plop, plop, plop, up the muddy path and up to the higher hills.

Three cheers for Agnes.

They found Al and Bell near some trees. They were really stuck in mud. The ranger said, "We'll make a train." He tied Bell to Al. Then he tied Al to Agnes. Then he got on Agnes and said, "Okay, Agnes, let's tow these horses back down to the barn."

It was not easy. Agnes had to strain hard. And at first, she didn't think she would be able to get the train started. But she kept straining, and slowly, the train went down the hills. It took a long time to get back to the barn because Al and Bell kept getting stuck. But at last they made it.

When the train of horses made it back to the barn, the horses shouted, "Three cheers for Agnes. Hip hip hooray. Hip hip hooray . . . ."

Agnes blushed and said, "Well . . . I . . . thank you."

More next time.

Two hundred bees wanted sweet butter. A farmer had sweet butter. So the bees said, "Let's go over to the farm and take that butter." They did not know that the farmer had made sweet cakes with his sweet butter. When the bees got to the farm, they did not find any butter. So they came back with five sweet cakes.

1. How many bees wanted sweet butter?

2. Who had that sweet butter?

3. What did the farmer make with the butter?

4. How many sweet cakes did the bees take?

1. scared
2. biting
3. game
4. spider
5. closer
6. saving

1. they are ⟶ they're
2. we are ⟶ we're
3. they would ⟶ they'd
4. he is ⟶ he's
5. it is ⟶ it's
6. I would ⟶ I'd

1. house
2. dart
3. brags
4. ground
5. dried

1. apple
2. growing
3. ashamed
4. buy
5. strong
6. eyes

The ranger should buy Agnes.

A Horse Named Agnes
Part Six

After the ranger left, Al told the other horses, "I am ashamed of myself. I called Agnes Big Foot and made fun of her because she couldn't run fast. But she is the best horse on this farm, and I'm going to let the ranger know that she is the horse he should buy."

The other horses nodded and said things like, "Yes, she's something else."

Agnes was so happy that she had big tears in her eyes.

I need a horse that is quick and strong.

A week later, the ranger returned to the farm. The mud was dried up, and the sun was out. The ranger and the farmer walked up to the barn. Al was ready to dart out of the barn and try to let the ranger know that Agnes was the best horse. But he stopped and listened to what the ranger was saying to the farmer.

"Well," the ranger said, "I really need two horses. I need one that is quick and strong. I've seen Al showing off, and I want him."

Before Al could do anything, the ranger went on. "I also need a mud horse," he said. "Your horse Agnes is the best mud horse I have ever seen. So I'd like to buy her, too."

... And Agnes is the best mud horse there is.

The horses inside the barn cheered. Al was smiling and laughing. Agnes was smiling and crying. And the ranger was happy because he felt that he had found two good horses.

The ranger has had those two horses for three years now, and they never let him down. The ranger brags a lot about them. He'll tell anybody who will listen that he has the best two horses a ranger could have.

The end.

Sam the snake wanted to eat a snail. But the snail had another plan. Just as Sam opened his lips to eat him, the snail slipped a hot pepper inside those lips. Sam yelled and darted away. He said, "I don't like to eat snails. They are too hot!"

1. What was Sam?

2. What did Sam try to eat?

3. What did the snail slip inside Sam's lips?

4. Who yelled and darted away?

ou aw

qu

1. horse
2. piles
3. time
4. broke
5. bite
6. driving

1. smelled
2. smiled
3. smallest
4. here
5. there
6. does

1. sound
2. ground
3. claw
4. clear
5. splash
6. eagle

1. pet
2. spot
3. beak
4. flap
5. sweet

Here Pig One.
Here Pig Two . . .

Peppers for Pam's Pigs

Pam had six pigs. Five pigs were big. The pig named Pig Six was very small.

One day, Pam didn't have pig food for them. All she had were piles of red hot peppers. She had never fed her pigs peppers, but she said, "I don't think these hot peppers will bother my pigs. Those pigs eat everything."

So she loaded some peppers in a pot and some peppers in a pan. She went to the pig pen with the pot and the pan of peppers. She set the peppers in a pile and called the pigs.

The pigs came and smelled the peppers. But they didn't start eating. Pam said, "I don't have pig food. Why don't you try eating these peppers?"

So the pigs started to eat. After ten seconds, all the pigs but one had turned red. Those pigs stopped eating and ran to the drinking pan at the other end of the pen and began to drink. The pigs drank and drank. Then those pigs ran here and there, eating dirt and trying to make the hot taste go away. Those pigs were still very red.

While the five pigs were rolling and eating dirt, the smallest pig was still eating and eating those hot peppers. She ate all the peppers, but she didn't turn red at all. She was just pink. Pam asked her, "Don't those peppers make you hot at all?"

The smallest pig made a little smile and then said, "Burp." That was her way of saying thank you.

The end.

Bob Went Sailing

Bob went out on a sail boat with three pals. The wind took the sail boat far, far away from shore. Then the wind stopped, and the boat stopped, too. Bob told his pals, "I have to be home by five."

One of his pals said, "How can we get back again if there is no wind?"

At last, the wind started blowing again, and the sail boat got back to shore. When Bob got home, it was after five.

1. What's the name of this story?

2. Did Bob and his pals go in a row boat or a sail boat?

3. How many pals went with Bob?

4. What did the sail boat do when the wind stopped?

5. Was Bob late when he got home?

1. kind
2. eagle
3. puddle
4. snuck
5. clear
6. slam

1. shouldn't
2. I'd
3. she's
4. it's
5. they've

1. spider
2. saving
3. closer
4. scared

1. chirp
2. spla<u>sh</u>
3. sw<u>oo</u>p
4. <u>sh</u>ock

1. <u>shocked</u>
2. <u>smiled</u>
3. <u>creeping</u>
4. <u>landed</u>
5. <u>wider</u>

The Little Bug Bites

A little bug was the best biting bug, but he didn't bite a lot. One time, he had to bite. He was playing with Jill, her brother, and her sister. They were on a stump, playing a game of jump. "I can jump far," Jill said. And she jumped from one side of the stump to the other side.

Her brother said, "I can do better than that." He jumped from one side of the stump and sailed over the other side.

The other bugs cheered. But when they saw where he landed, they were shocked. He was in a spider web. "Help, help," he called. "I'm stuck in this web."

A big spider was not far away, and that spider was creeping closer to Jill's brother. Jill's brother was scared, and so was Jill. She said, "What can we do?"

The little bug said, "We can do some big time biting." He jumped down into the web and started to bite a hole in the web. He told Jill's brother, "Jump down into this hole, and you will be safe."

Then the little bug looked at the spider and said, "Stay back, or I will take a big bite out of you."

The spider smiled and said, "You make me laugh. Show me your best bite."

The little bug showed his teeth and said, "This is how my bite starts out. Then I open wide and roar like this."

The bug opened up so wide and made such a big roar that it almost sent the spider flying.

That spider ran and hid while the little bug and Jill's brother got out of the web.

After the bugs were safe, Jill gave the little bug a big hug and thanked him for saving her brother.

The end.

brown   cow

Two bugs jumped on a horse that was walking down the road. When the horse got to the zoo, they jumped off and went inside. They had a wonderful time at the zoo. They saw apes and lions and tigers and baboons. They saw a moose, and they saw a goose. They had so much fun that only one of those bugs went home at the end of the day. The other bug stayed in the lion's den.

1. How many bugs went to the zoo?

2. Write each name that tells about things the bugs saw.

   •tigers   •fish   •apes   •lions   •baboons
   •toads   •moose   •snakes   •goose   •crows

3. Did they have a good time?

4. How many bugs went home?

5. Where did the bug that did not go home stay?

1. own
2. yum yum
3. pet
4. spotted
5. slammed

1. across
2. careful
3. helpless
4. clearly
5. whenever

1. Bonnie
2. Sweetie
3. fence
4. thought
5. kinds

1. watching
2. splashing
3. chirping
4. swooping
5. flapping
6. wondering

Those birds need
a bird bath.

Sweetie and the Bird Bath
Part One

Bonnie really liked birds. One day, she saw
some birds cleaning themselves by splashing in a
puddle. She said to herself, "Those birds shouldn't
have to take a bath in a puddle. They should have
a bird bath."

She kept thinking about the bird bath. She liked
that plan. She said to herself, "I'll buy a big bird
bath. It will be so big that any bird who needs to
get clean can come to my yard and jump in the bird
bath."

Yum, yum.

So Bonnie went to the pet store and got the biggest bird bath they had. She set up that bird bath in her yard. And soon, birds started to gather in the bird bath. These birds called to their pals, and before long, the bird bath was filled with all kinds of birds—yellow birds, red birds, brown birds, and spotted birds.

Bonnie watched all these birds, but she wasn't the only one watching them. A big yellow cat lived next do<u>or</u>. That cat's name was Sweetie, but that cat wasn't sweet at all. When Sweetie saw all those birds, he said to himself, "Yum, yum."

As Sweetie watched and watched, he made up a plan. He said to himself, "I will sneak over to that bird bath. Then I will jump up before the birds know I am around. I'll grab two or three of them before they can get out of the water. Yum, yum."

More to come.

yellow	black	play

Don was a cook who was very neat. He cooked at a pla<u>ce</u> called the Fry Shop. Did Don leave batter on the pots and pans? No. Did Don leave dirty cups in the sink? No. What did Don do at the end of each day? Don cleaned up the pots and pans in the sink.

1. Where did Don cook?

2. Was Don a neat cook?

3. Did Don leave batter on things?

4. When did Don clean up the pots and pans?

N

1. b<u>ea</u>k
2. str<u>ea</u>k
3. s<u>ou</u>nds
4. m<u>ou</u>th
5. cl<u>aws</u>
6. <u>ouch</u>

W

1. <u>painted</u>
2. <u>flapping</u>
3. <u>clearly</u>
4. <u>swooped</u>
5. <u>chirping</u>
6. <u>slammed</u>

E

1. weak
2. bunch
3. park
4. snuck
5. spends

1. fen<u>ce</u>
2. care<u>f</u>ul
3. th<u>ought</u>
4. eagle
5. own

S

I am ready.

Sweetie and the Bird Bath
Part Two

Sweetie had a plan. And he was ready to start doing what he planned.

He snuck into Bonnie's yard. He went into some long grass near the fence. Very slowly, he snuck closer and closer to the bird bath. He was careful not to make a sound. At last, he was almost under the bird bath. He was now ready to leap up and grab two or three birds.

But just as he was ready to spring up, he heard a lot of flapping sounds and chirping. Sweetie stopped and waited for the birds to quiet down.

Sweetie couldn't see the top of the bird bath. So he didn't see why all the birds were chirping and flapping their wings. Sweetie didn't know that an eagle had swooped down to take a bath. When the other birds saw the eagle swooping down with its big claws and sharp beak, they took off. Those birds left the bird bath as fast as their little wings could take them.

splash

Ouch.

Things were <u>qu</u>iet now. Sweetie th t that
the little birds were still in the bird bath. So he got
<u>rea</u>dy to spring up and grab two or three little
birds. He didn't know that there were no little birds
in that bird bath. There was only one bird—an
eagle that was about three times as big as Sweetie.

Sweetie took a big leap. He landed on one side
of the bird bath. He landed with his claws out,
grabbing at the first thing he could reach. Things
happened so fast that Sweetie really didn't see the
eagle clearly. He grabbed the eagle, and in less
than a second, the eagle grabbed him with its big
claws. The eagle picked Sweetie up and slammed
him down in the bird bath. Splash. <u>Ou</u>ch.

More next time.

| closed | window | door |

49

218

Henry was an ant. He was very scared of spiders. He was scared of their long legs and the way they jumped. Henry didn't like the sticky webs they made. Most of all, he was scared of getting stuck in a web.

Henry th t, "There are no webs in my ant hill. I will stay home." So Henry cleaned and served other ants at the ant hill. Other ants left the ant hill to gather seeds.

1. What was Henry?

2. Who didn't like spiders?

3. What was Henry most scared of?

4. Where did Henry stay?

5. What did other ants do when they left the ant hill?